Kids Making a Difference

Overcoming Personal Challenges

Vic Parker

Chicago, Illinois

www.capstonepub.com
Visit our website to find out more information about Heinemann-Raintree books.

To order:

☎ Phone 800-747-4992

💻 Visit www.capstonepub.com to browse our catalog and order online.

Edited by Nancy Dickmann and Laura Knowles
Designed by Victoria Allen
Picture research by Mica Brančić
Illustrations by HL Studios

Originated by Capstone Global Library, Ltd
Printed and bound in China by CTPS

16 15 14 13 12
10 9 8 7 6 5 4 3 2 1

Library of Congress Cataloging-in-Publication Data
Parker, Victoria.
  Overcoming personal challenges / Vic Parker.
    p. cm.—(Kids making a difference)
  Includes bibliographical references and index.
  ISBN 978-1-4329-6503-7 (hb)—ISBN 978-1-4329-6508-2 (pb)
1. Determination (Personality trait) in children—Case studies—Juvenile literature. 2. Children with social disabilities—Case studies—Juvenile literature. 3. Children with disabilities—Case studies—Juvenile literature. 4. Achievement motivation in children—Case studies—Juvenile literature. 5. Success in children—Case studies—Juvenile literature. I. Title.
  BF698.35.D48P37 2013
  155.2'4—dc23   2011039443

Acknowledgments
The author and publisher are grateful to the following for permission to reproduce copyright material: Corbis pp. 4 (Tetra Images/© Erik Isakson), 5 (© Reuters/Juda Ngwenya), 7 (isiphotos.com/ © Michael Janosz), 11 (© Jerry Cooke), 12 (© Image Source), 23 (Demotix/© Arindam Dey), 31 (Science Faction/© Ed Darack); Getty Images pp. 13 (WireImage/Chelsea Lauren), 35 (Hamish Blair), 40 (Photoshot); Kids Rights pp. 24, 26, 27 (Kimberly Gomes); Library of Congress p. 15 (Prints and Photographs Division Washington, D.C.); Newscom p. 41 (UPI Photo/Roger L. Wollenberg); Newscom/The Daily Mirror p. 17 (Mike Moore); Photoshot p. 19 (© UPPA); Press Association Images pp. 36 (PA Archive/Michael Stephens), 38 (PA Archive/Andrew Matthews), 39 (PA Archive/Andrew Matthews); Reuters p. 29 (© STR New); Rex Features p. 21; Shutterstock p. 16 (© prism68); Stronghead Fellowship pp. 30 (Zoë Adams); 33 (Zoë Adams); Superstock p. 8 (© Kablonk).

Cover photograph of teenage girls playing cards, one with disability and a scar from open-heart surgery, reproduced with permission of Getty Images/Huntstock.

Background design images supplied by Shutterstock/Toria/ZeroTO/silver-john.

Every effort has been made to contact copyright holders of material reproduced in this book. Any omissions will be rectified in subsequent printings if notice is given to the publisher.

Disclaimer
All the Internet addresses (URLs) given in this book were valid at the time of going to press. However, due to the dynamic nature of the Internet, some addresses may have changed, or sites may have changed or ceased to exist since publication. While the author and publisher regret any inconvenience this may cause readers, no responsibility for any such changes can be accepted by either the author or the publisher.

Contents

In their own words
Look for these boxes to find inspirational quotes from the kids featured in this book and other famous people who made a difference.

Kids who made a difference

These boxes tell you stories about kids who have done great things to make the world a better place, both now and in the past.

Top tips

Search for these boxes for quick facts about how you can make a difference.

Some words in the book are in bold, **like this**. You can find out what they mean by looking in the glossary.

What Are Personal Challenges?

Personal challenges are difficult conditions or situations that we have to deal with as we go through life. We all share certain personal challenges, such as starting at a new school, making friends, or getting good grades. However, we all have individual personal challenges to face, too. These may be things like being scared of the dark, being in foster care, or having a medical condition. What personal challenges do you face?

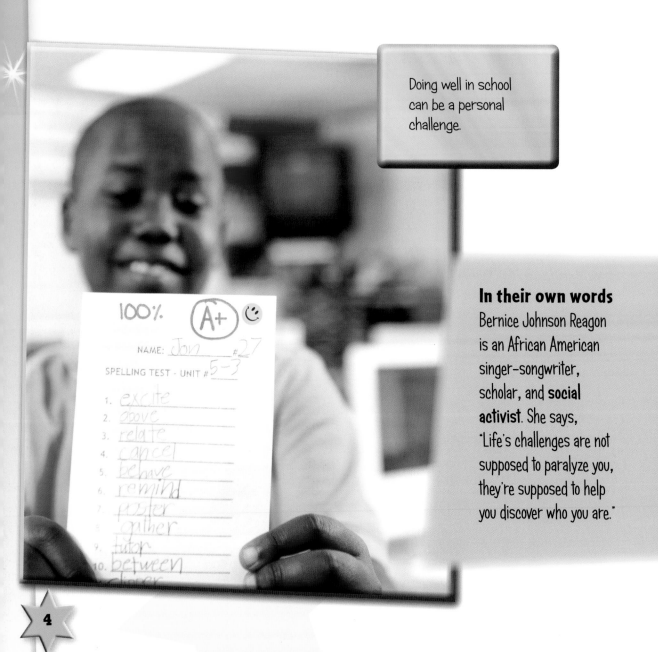

Doing well in school can be a personal challenge.

In their own words
Bernice Johnson Reagon is an African American singer-songwriter, scholar, and **social activist**. She says, "Life's challenges are not supposed to paralyze you, they're supposed to help you discover who you are."

A challenge from the start

Some people are born with personal challenges to overcome. For instance, millions of children all over the world are born into areas suffering from **poverty** or war. Many others are born with learning difficulties or physical problems.

Kids who made a difference

Nkosi Johnson was born in 1989 in South Africa with a life-threatening virus, **HIV/AIDS**. His mother had passed the illness on to him. She was a single parent, and by the time Nkosi was two, she was too sick to care for him, so he was adopted. Nkosi and his foster mother worked hard to improve life for children like him. They fought for the right to go to school and for free drugs. Nkosi died when he was 12, but was awarded the International Children's Peace Prize.

Nkosi gave a speech to thousands at the 13th International AIDS Conference in 2000.

Coping with sudden hardship

For some people, personal challenges come out of the blue. They might have to deal with their family falling on hard times, perhaps when a parent loses his or her job. They might have to cope with their parents splitting up or the death of a loved one. Sudden illness or injury can present a real challenge. So can moving to a new home in a different area.

A challenge or an opportunity?

We all find different things challenging. And everyone feels sad, frustrated, and overwhelmed from time to time. It is important to find a way to deal with your feelings and put them behind you, so they do not drag you down. There are many places to get help and advice when dealing with difficult times.

If you face a personal challenge with a positive attitude and **determination**, you can achieve great success and inspire others along the way. Read on to meet some young people who have done exactly that!

Kids who made a difference

Bethany Hamilton was born in 1990 in Hawaii. She is a talented young surfer. When she was 13, a tiger shark ripped off her left arm in a rare attack. Such a terrible injury might have stopped many people from going back into the ocean, but less than a month later she was back on her surfboard. Since then, she has won many awards, and she now surfs on the U.S. national team.

Bethany Hamilton has inspired thousands of young people with her courage and determination.

In their own words
Albert Einstein was a German-born, Nobel Prize–winning scientist. He once said, "In the middle of every difficulty lies opportunity."

Jaylen Arnold: Beating Bullies

Being bullied is awful. Bullies pick on people on purpose and repeatedly. Bullies might call people names, say or write nasty things about them, or leave them out of activities or conversations. Sometimes they threaten them, take or damage their belongings, or make them do things they do not want to do. Some bullies even hit or kick people.

Some bullies hurt others to make themselves look tough or to get attention. Others do it out of jealousy. A few do it just because they have been bullied themselves. Most people who are bullied get picked on for no particular reason. But sometimes bullies pick on something that stands out about a person.

It is normal to be different. Being different from others makes us who we are.

Meet Jaylen Arnold

One person who knows all about bullying is Jaylen Arnold, who was born in 2000. Jaylen, who lives in Florida, has **disabilities** that make him an easy target for bullies. But instead of being beaten down by it, Jaylen has become an anti-bullying hero.

Jaylen lives in Lakeland, Florida, shown here.

CANADA

UNITED STATES

New York

Washington D.C.

Los Angeles

PACIFIC OCEAN

N

ATLANTIC OCEAN

Lakeland FLORIDA

GULF OF MEXICO

MEXICO

0   500 miles

0   500 kilometers

In their own words

The U.S. businessman Harvey S. Firestone said, "Never be bullied into silence. Never allow yourself to be made a victim. Accept no one's definition of your life, but define yourself."

A toddler with tics

By the age of three, Jaylen was diagnosed with Tourette's Syndrome. This condition causes people's brain and nerves to "misfire" sometimes, sending the wrong messages to the body. This makes them do things such as roll their eyes, jerk their head, or punch the air. These things are called physical tics. People with Tourette's can also make noises or shout out words. These are called vocal tics.

People cannot "catch" Tourette's. It also does not affect a person's intelligence. Many people with Tourette's are very smart, like Jaylen. But there is no cure for the tics, which are very noticeable.

Other challenges

Many people with Tourette's have other conditions to cope with, besides tics. Jaylen had to deal with Obsessive Compulsive Disorder (OCD) as well. This is a condition that makes people fixated on certain thoughts and behaviors. Jaylen was obsessed with keeping free of germs. He performed certain **rituals**, such as hand washing, over and over again, every day.

At age eight, Jaylen was also diagnosed with Asperger's Syndrome. This is a condition in which people have difficulties with communication and social skills. For instance, they may not be able to read body language or understand another person's feelings.

Top tips

Have you ever been mean to someone on purpose? Maybe you thought you were being funny or trying to fit in with your friends. To avoid hurting others, always think about how you would feel if someone said or did something mean to you.

Wilma Rudolph leads the way in a race at the 1960 Olympics. She won individual gold medals in both the 100- and 200-meter races.

Kids who made a difference

Wilma Rudolph was born in Clarksville, Tennessee, in 1940, into an African American family. Her family was very poor. When she was just four years old, Wilma caught a disease called polio. It left her with a crippled leg, but she made up her mind she would walk again. By high school, Wilma was a star basketball player. She went on to win three Olympic gold medals for running and set up an organization to support young athletes.

Taking a stand

Mr. and Mrs. Arnold paid for Jaylen to go to a special **private school** with other children with disabilities, where everyone understood and accepted each other. However, when Jaylen was seven, he decided he wanted to go to a **mainstream** school. Sadly, he was bullied for being "weird." The bullying was so awful, it made Jaylen's tics very bad. He was sore and exhausted from all the jerking and was extremely upset.

Jaylen returned to his special school, where he was much happier. But he did not let the bullies get the better of him. Jaylen returned to see them and explained about his conditions. The bullies apologized. Encouraged by this, Jaylen began a campaign called Jaylen's Challenge, with its own website, to raise awareness about bullying. He began giving anti-bullying presentations at schools and handing out anti-bullying packets he had made.

It is never nice to feel bullied or left out. If you see someone being treated unkindly, do not join in. Instead, let the person know that you are on his or her side.

Turning a negative into a positive

Jaylen's courage inspired several celebrities to support his campaign, including Hollywood actors Leonardo DiCaprio and Dash Mihok. Dash also has Tourette's. Jaylen has spoken at schools across the United States, appeared on television many times, and won several awards. He is determined to keep going, to stop as many bullies as possible.

Actor Dash Mihok can control his tics long enough to film a scene.

Top tips

If someone you know is being bullied, stick up for the person. Ask him or her what is happening—just being listened to can help make a person feel more confident. Then tell an adult you trust, even if your friend does not want you to. This is the best help you can give to your friend.

To learn more about his project, visit Jaylen's website at www.jaylenschallenge.org.

Nicole Dryburgh: Triumphing over Cancer and Disability

Blind people cannot see, but they can hear the world around them. Deaf people cannot hear, but they can see. But some people are both deaf and blind. The only way they can sense the world is by touch, smell, and taste.

Can you imagine becoming both deaf and blind? This is what happened to a girl named Nicole Dryburgh when she got **cancer**. But that did not stop her from achieving amazing things!

Meet Nicole

Nicole Dryburgh was born in 1989 in Glasgow, Scotland. When she was seven, her parents separated, and she went with her mother and older brother, Lee, to live in Whitstable, England. Nicole was very active. She loved walking her two dogs and doing gymnastics. However, when she was 11 years old, she was diagnosed with a **tumor** at the top of her spine (backbone). She was sick with a rare kind of cancer.

> Nicole Dryburgh was born in Scotland but spent most of her life in the south of England.

A terrible blow

Nicole had to have a lot of hospital treatments, which shrunk the tumor. However, just two years later, she suddenly collapsed. This turned out to be because another tumor was growing. Nicole spent over three months in the hospital before she was well enough to return home, but she had become blind and unable to walk.

Helen Keller's teacher, Anne Sullivan, was **visually impaired**.

Kids who made a difference

Helen Keller was born in 1880 in Tuscumbia, Alabama. At 19 months old, she had an illness that left her deaf and blind. At age seven, Helen's parents employed a teacher for her, Anne Sullivan, who taught Helen to communicate by spelling words into her hand. Helen grew up to be the first deaf and blind person to gain a college degree, and she became a world-famous speaker and author.

Fighting spirit

Doctors had told Nicole and her family that she did not have long to live. However, Nicole made up her mind to prove everyone wrong. She decided to strengthen her back and legs so she could try to walk again, so she learned how to ride horses with the Riding for the Disabled Association. She learned how to read a system of raised bumps, called Braille, using her fingertips. She also learned how to touch-type on a laptop that could "talk" to her.

The system of raised bumps that blind people can read by touch is called Braille.

This is a picture of Nicole with her mom. Jackie. taken in 2008.

Helping others

Nicole was determined to help other young people in similar situations. She began **fund-raising** by organizing events like yard sales. She did **sponsored** events and sold copies of poems she had written. She also sold cards and decorations. Touch-in-art lessons at her special needs school helped her to make these things. Nicole made hundreds of dollars, and she **donated** it to charities that help sick children. One of the charities she supported was the Demelza House **Hospice**, where she had received treatment.

Top tips

If you have a serious health crisis, it can be really helpful to talk to other young people with the same condition. Your doctor or nurse may be able to put you in touch. You can share your ups and downs and give each other support.

Living a full life

Nicole's illness taught her to make the most of every moment. She did many fun things, such as swimming with dolphins and flying a glider plane! She decided she wanted to be a journalist and enrolled in a program to study English. And she continued to fight for her health. Amazingly, in April 2006, Nicole walked a few steps without any assistance, in water in a treatment pool.

Nicole also continued to raise funds and awareness for sick young people. She appeared on television shows, had **extracts** from her diary published in a national newspaper, and set up her own website. She won awards for bravery and became known for her courage. But when she was 17, both tumors started growing again, and Nicole had to go through more treatment.

Top tips

If you are feeling down about things, there are some actions you can take to help yourself feel better:

• Let your family or friends know how you are feeling or write your thoughts down.

• Take part in a sport or type of exercise that you enjoy. Exercise can make your mind feel better as well as your body.

To learn more about her inspiring story, visit Nicole's website at www.c-h-o-c.org.uk.

Even more challenges to face

Once again, the treatment shrunk Nicole's spine tumors. She celebrated her 18th birthday, a day everyone had thought she would never see. But more health problems lay in store. In January 2007, Nicole began finding it hard to hear and, by August, doctors had found tumors in her ears. By the time Nicole was 19, she had lost most of her hearing. She and all her family and friends had to learn deaf–blind sign language, in order to communicate.

Nicole's family and friends used a system of signing into her hand to communicate with her.

Ambitions achieved

In January 2008, a dream came true for Nicole: she had a book published, called *The Way I See It*. Nicole had been writing it since she was 15. It was the story of her life with cancer. She wanted it to help people in situations similar to what she faced, by showing that people should never give up hope.

Nicole put all the money from the sales of the book toward her fund-raising. She wanted to raise money for Kings College Hospital, where she had received a lot of treatment. She even raised money by **rappelling** down the hospital building! By mid-2008, she had raised enough to pay for a special room for children recovering from severe brain and spinal injuries. It was called "Nicole's Sweet," after her love of chocolate. Nicole won a Britain's Most Inspiring Fund-Raiser award for her incredible efforts. She immediately set herself a new target to raise $150,000 for the Teenage Cancer Trust.

In their own words
Helen Keller once said, "Although the world is full of suffering, it is also full of the overcoming of it."

An inspirational life

Nicole raised over $113,000 for the Teenage Cancer Trust, but she did not meet her target because, sadly, she died suddenly of bleeding in her brain in 2010. She was just 21. You can read about all the awards she won during the last years of her life in a second book she had published, called *Talk to the Hand*. Even though Nicole is gone, thousands of people are still raising money for her fund in her name. Her life really did make a difference.

Nicole was extremely proud of being a published author.

Om Prakash Gurjar: From Slavery to Saving Others

Many parts of the world celebrate the fact that they have **abolished slavery**, but there are still places where slavery is a part of everyday life for thousands of people. One slave was Om Prakash Gurjar, who was born in a village in India in 1992. Om Prakash was one of eleven children, and his family was very poor. His father once borrowed money but was unable to pay it back. So the moneylender took Om Prakash away to work for him instead. This was a common practice, even though it has been illegal (against the law) in India since 1976. Om Prakash was just five years old.

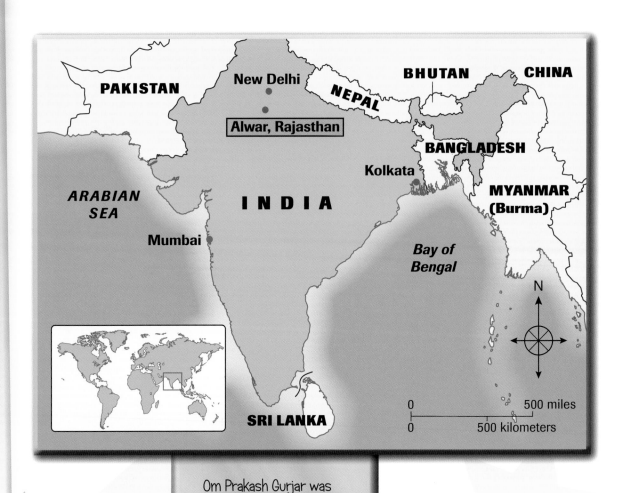

Om Prakash Gurjar was raised in a part of India called Rajasthan.

Suffering in slavery

For three years, Om Prakash worked long hours every day on a farm. He worked hard at herding cattle, plowing, sowing seeds, harvesting, and handling dangerous chemicals. He was given just two meals a day and no pay. If he ever made a mistake, his master would beat him.

Millions of children around the world have to work. Some of them do not have any choice.

Kids who made a difference

James Kofi Annan was born in Ghana, a country in West Africa, in 1974. His father sold James into slavery in exchange for a money loan when he was six. He worked in fishing villages for seven years, then escaped. He taught himself to read and write and was accepted into a college. He has since opened his own school for former child slaves and become a world leader in the fight against child slavery.

Rescued!

At the age of eight, Om Prakash was rescued by people from an organization that was set up to find and free child slaves. He went to live at the Bal Ashram rescue center, where he was fed and received medical care. Om Prakash was able to go to school and could visit his family regularly.

Om Prakash talked to other children about what he had been through. He realized that there were thousands of young people in India and other countries who had been enslaved, just like him. He made up his mind to do what he could to help.

About 100 rescued child slaves live at the Bal Ashram rescue center.

Standing up for children's rights

By the age of 12, Om Prakash had become head of the school's student council. When the school announced that all students would have to pay tuition fees, Om Prakash took a stand. He knew that most children were too poor to afford fees, and he also knew it was against the law. The school was a government school and supposed to be free. Om Prakash made a protest in the local court and won a huge victory for thousands of poor children. From then on, no government school in the whole state would be allowed to charge fees.

Top tips

If there is an issue you feel strongly about, research it at the library or online to make sure you know the facts. If you would like to take a stand against something you feel is unfair, you could raise people's awareness by making posters and buttons. You could make a storybook or put on a play. You could set up or join a **petition** and e-mail the people in charge of the situation. Everyone can make a difference!

A new campaign

Many poor Indian families did not **register** children's births because it cost money. Without a **birth certificate**, these children did not officially exist. They grew up without any protection against slavery, **forced marriage**, or being made to fight as child soldiers. They could not access health care or education. As adults, they could not vote.

Om Prakash began traveling, visiting schools and villages to convince hundreds of people to register their children. Om Prakash also persuaded everyone in his home village to ban child labor and announced that the village was a "Bal Mitra Gram," or a Child Friendly Village. Then he worked hard to do the same in other villages.

Om Prakash poses with former child slaves.

In 2006, Om Prakash was awarded the International Children's Peace Prize.

In their own words
Nelson Mandela has spent his life fighting for racial equality and was president of South Africa from 1994 to 1999. He once said, "To be free is not merely to cast off one's chains, but to live in a way that respects and enhances the freedom of others."

Lovetta Conto: Building Success Out of War and Bereavement

Liberia is a country in West Africa. War broke out there in 1989, but it was not a conflict with another country. Instead, it was a **civil war**, in which the people of Liberia fought each other to see which of two leaders should become president. The fighting was not just between armies and soldiers—neighbors began fighting each other, too. Everyone was caught up in the conflict, whether they wanted to be or not, including a little girl named Lovetta Conto.

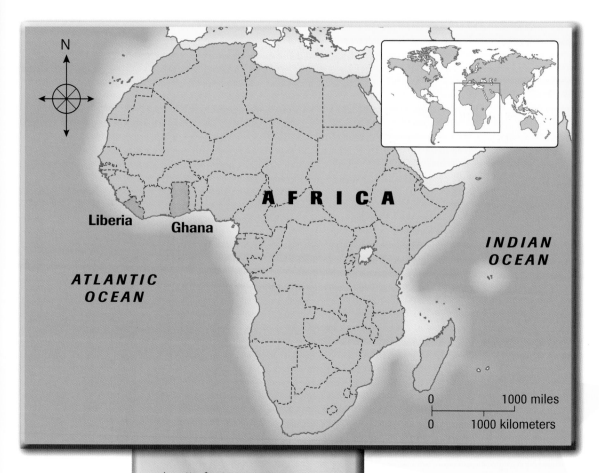

Lovetta Conto was born in Liberia, West Africa, and lived for several years in Ghana.

Escape

Lovetta was born in 1992. She was just four when soldiers attacked her town. Her mother was out, so Lovetta's father, Larry, scooped Lovetta up and fled into the countryside. All they had were the clothes they were wearing. Larry later searched and searched for Lovetta's mother, but he could not find her. Sadly, he had to assume she had been killed. Larry and Lovetta walked for a week, hiding from soldiers and sleeping outside, until they crossed into the country of Ghana.

When Larry and Lovetta reached Ghana, they made their way to a camp that had been set up for Liberian **refugees**. There were around 47,000 refugees in the camp. At first, Lovetta and her dad slept on a plastic sheet on the ground. Later, they found a shared tent to live in. Food and water were always scarce, but they tried to get on with their lives.

Top tips

There are many charities that assist refugees. You can help them by donating items refugees can use, such as clothes, shoes, books, blankets, toys, or money that you have raised.

Refugee camps are crowded places where living conditions are rough.

29

Lovetta's courage shines through

Larry tried to find work, so that he could pay for Lovetta to go to school. When she did attend school, she was often beaten for not wearing a uniform or having any books. But she was determined to make her future brighter and also to improve the lives of other refugees.

Lovetta Conto is a girl with great spirit and determination.

Lovetta worked with some U.S. volunteers to build a school for refugee children. She also spoke up for children with sight problems for the right to go to school. A U.S. woman, Cori Stern, noticed Lovetta's efforts. She had set up an organization to find gifted young people affected by war and give them the chance of a new life. Cori worked for two years to get Lovetta documents to travel to the United States. Finally, when Lovetta was 14, she said goodbye to her father and went off to make a new future.

An inspired idea

Cori's organization, the Strongheart Fellowship, wanted to set Lovetta up in a business that would give her a living, while also helping others. At first Lovetta thought of being a lawyer, but her heart lay in fashion and design. Lovetta thought of making jewelry from the casings, or outer shells, of bullets used in the Liberian civil war. Each piece was inscribed with the word "life." She called her line Akawelle, which means "Also known as love."

Around 250,000 people were killed in Liberia's civil war. Lovetta made her jewelry out of bullet casings like these.

From hardship to success

By 2011, Lovetta's beautiful, meaningful jewelry was being worn by people all over the world, including other children in refugee camps and celebrities, such as the Hollywood actress Hilary Swank. Lovetta used the profits from her business to create a home in Liberia called Strongheart House. This is a place where she and other young people involved in the Strongheart program can live. Lovetta was reunited with her father and also her mother, whom they discovered had survived the war after all.

Awards and plans

Lovetta has used her experiences of hardship and success to reach out to thousands of people in many countries. She has traveled all over the world to speak at conferences, her story has been featured on television, and she has appeared in newspapers. She was one of the finalists for the International Children's Peace Prize in 2008.

Lovetta always believes that anything is possible, and she has plans for another project to inspire young people. She wants to create a magazine for young African teenagers, which will give information on health and social issues as well as entertain readers.

In their own words
The U.S. author and journalist Ernest Hemingway once said, "The world breaks us all and, after, some are stronger in the broken places."

To learn more about Lovetta's story and see her jewelry, visit her website at www.akawelle.com.

Kids who made a difference

Ishmael Beah was born in 1980 in the West African country of Sierra Leone. At the age of 12 he was forced to become a soldier in a civil war. He was rescued three years later by workers from an aid organization called UNICEF. Ishmael went to live in the United States, where he rebuilt his life. Now he speaks out against the use of children as soldiers. He has published books, spoken at the United Nations, and worked with world leaders such as Bill Clinton and Nelson Mandela.

Since surviving the civil war in Liberia. Lovetta Conto has helped thousands of people in a similar situation.

Darius Knight: From the Ghetto to Gold Medals

Darius Knight was born in 1990 in the United Kingdom. His family lived in the capital city, London. Darius grew up in a poor part of the city. He lived in a public housing area made up of cramped apartment buildings surrounded by run-down stores and factories. There was nothing for young people to do. By the age of 10, Darius spent most of his time roaming the streets. He hung out with people who were in **gangs** and took drugs. It looked like that was going to be his future, too.

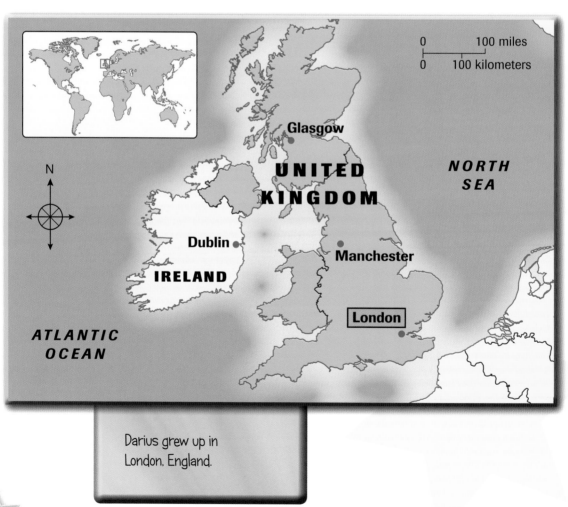

0   100 miles
0   100 kilometers

Glasgow

UNITED KINGDOM

NORTH SEA

N

Dublin

Manchester

IRELAND

London

ATLANTIC OCEAN

Darius grew up in London, England.

A lucky step

Darius's life changed when he was 11 years old. He happened to wander into a youth club and pick up a table tennis (Ping-Pong) paddle. He had never played table tennis before and was the worst player there. But a coach named Gideon Ashison gave him some tips and encouragement. Darius became hooked on the game. He spent every available minute practicing table tennis, trying to get faster and more accurate.

Top tips

You don't know which sport you might enjoy or be good at unless you try! There are some programs that offer sports for free, and other clubs will let you try a sport for free, to see if you like it. So go ahead and try some different sports out. You will make new friends, get fitter, become more confident, have fun, and maybe even improve your life, too.

Darius discovered he loved the feeling of winning!

Moving onward and upward

Darius was thrilled when Coach Ashison picked him as one of the best players at the youth club to have extra practice sessions. When Ashison lost use of the practice hall, he managed to find a large backyard shed that the kids could use instead. The only problem was that it was over an hour away. But Darius and the other gifted young players were not discouraged. They were too busy winning trophies in major competitions. At the 2001 Greater London Championships, 11-year-old Darius won the under-12, under-14, and under-17 categories.

Darius's success has brought a lot of media attention. Here. he plays table tennis with teammate Paul Drinkhall at the London Eye for a newspaper article in 2008.

A golden opportunity

In September 2002, a major UK newspaper, *The Times*, ran a story about the inner-city children who were becoming sports stars from a backyard shed. Readers sent donations totaling $16,000 to support the young players. Darius, his teammates, and Ashison were stunned. Suddenly, they could afford to train at a multi-table sports hall in a community college. They even bought a state-of-the-art table tennis robot, which lets players practice by firing balls at them that they can hit back. There was also enough left over to set up a project operating tennis table programs in seven inner-city London schools.

Kids who made a difference

In 1961, Li Cunxin was born into poverty in the People's Republic of China. At the age of 11, he seized the opportunity to have a better future when he won a place at the prestigious Beijing Dance Academy. Li became a famous ballet star and performed in the United States before settling in Australia. Li's life story has been published as a children's book and also made into a movie, both called *Mao's Last Dancer*.

Blood, sweat, and tears

When Darius was 14 years old, coaches invited him to live and train at the National Training Center in Nottingham, England, a city about three hours from London. His mom, a struggling single parent with another young child, was not able to support his table tennis. She could not even afford to travel to watch him play at competitions. So Darius jumped at the chance to focus solely on his sport, surrounded by people who would help him. By the age of 16, Darius was the UK National Under-21 Champion.

Darius won a gold medal at the Australian Youth Olympics Festival in 2007.

To follow his career, visit Darius's website at www.dariusknight.com.

A shining example

Darius suffered a setback in 2008, when funding for the national table tennis team was cut. However, he did not give up. In 2010, at the age of 21, he won a silver medal as part of England's **Commonwealth Games** table tennis team in New Delhi, India. Darius has become the face of the Fred Perry Urban Cup, a program that helps promote sports for inner-city children, and he is now a role model for kids in underprivileged areas. He has a huge fan base of young people who want to follow in his footsteps.

Darius aims to win a gold medal at the 2012 Olympic Games in his home city of London.

You Can Make a Difference

Table tennis star Darius Knight has said, "You are always in control of your own **destiny**." The young people in this book who have overcome huge personal challenges have all been able to picture what they want to achieve, and they have had the imagination to think it is possible. They have not let anyone say, "No, you can't."

Kids who made a difference

Eleanor Simmonds was born in 1994 in Walsall, England. She has a medical condition called achondroplasia, which means that she will only ever grow to around 4 feet (123 centimeters) tall. She has become a star swimmer and won two gold medals at the 2008 Paralympics in China.

In 2009, Ellie Simmonds won an award from the British queen called an MBE. She is the youngest person ever to have received this.

Think big

You don't need to wait for difficult times to do great things. You can set yourself personal challenges today. Write yourself a list of goals. These can be things like making new friends, learning a new skill, passing a test, or fund-raising. Then write down what you need to do to meet these challenges. Who knows what you can do unless you try?

Kids who made a difference

Mawi Asgedom was born in 1976 in Ethiopia. He and his family escaped from a terrible war by trekking through the desert. They spent three years in a refugee camp, before traveling to the United States. Mawi educated himself and went on to graduate from Harvard University. Today, he is a best-selling author and **motivational speaker**.

Oprah Winfrey has said, "After I heard Mawi's story on the show, I wouldn't tolerate 'can't' from anyone."

Making a Difference Map

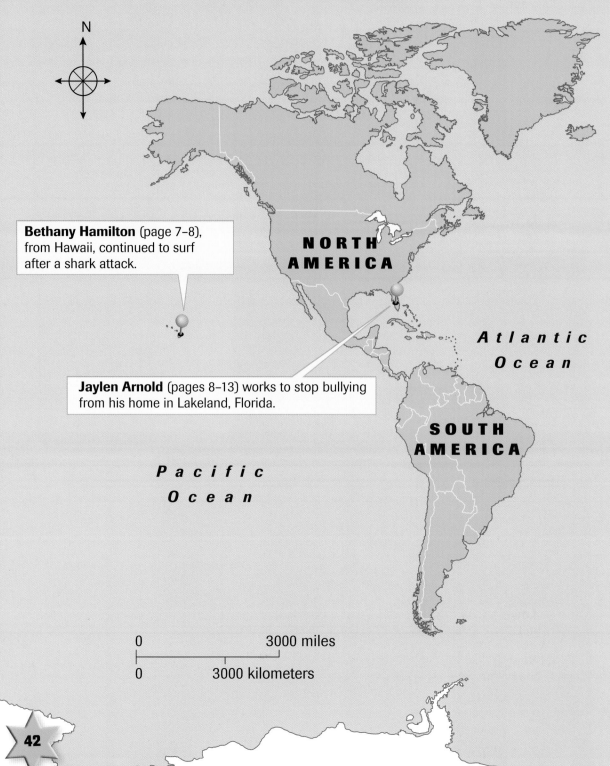

Arctic Ocean

N

NORTH AMERICA

Bethany Hamilton (page 7–8), from Hawaii, continued to surf after a shark attack.

Atlantic Ocean

Jaylen Arnold (pages 8–13) works to stop bullying from his home in Lakeland, Florida.

SOUTH AMERICA

Pacific Ocean

0   3000 miles

0   3000 kilometers

Arctic Ocean

Ellie Simmonds (page 40) was born in Walsall, England, and became a Paralympic star.

Darius Knight (pages 34–39) grew up in London and became a top table tennis player.

ASIA

Nicole Dryburgh (pages 14–21) lived in Whitstable, Kent, England, where she raised money for cancer charities.

EUROPE

Om Prakash Gurjar (pages 22–27) works to help child workers in Rajasthan, India.

Pacific Ocean

AFRICA

Mawi Asgedom (page 41) escaped war in Ethiopia and works to help others be the best they can be.

James Kofi Annan (page 23) fights child slavery in Ghana.

Indian Ocean

AUSTRALIA

Nkosi Johnson (page 5) lived in Johannesburg, South Africa, where he worked to help HIV-positive children.

Lovetta Conto (pages 28–33) escaped civil war in Liberia to start a successful jewelry line.

Ishmael Beah (page 33) was a child soldier in Sierra Leone before working to help others.

Southern Ocean

ANTARCTICA

Tips on Making a Difference

Overcoming personal challenges can be tough. Here are a few tips to get you started:

To overcome any personal challenge, you need:

* imagination—to picture how you can deal with your personal challenge

* a positive attitude—to believe "I can and I will" instead of "I can't and I won't be able to"

* determination—to stand up for yourself, even if others don't believe in you or if your situation seems hopeless

* courage—to open up about your problems and ask for help, and to grab or create opportunities that might support you

* strength—to keep going when the going gets tough.

These qualities can help you overcome personal challenges both big and small. Your example may also inspire others to achieve great things, too.

How to make a difference for others

Do you know anyone going through a difficult time? Do your best to offer support and encouragement. You can also help others by volunteering, or offering your time and help to a good cause. The help you give might be hands-on assistance, such as serving at a soup kitchen for the homeless, or helping to raise money, such as doing a sponsored run. By volunteering, you can make the world a better, happier place. Volunteering can also give you the chance to meet new friends, learn new skills, and have fun!

Choosing a charity

It is important to research a charity before you donate your money or time. An adult can help you do this. Here are some tips:

* First, find a charity that helps a cause you are interested in. Websites such as www.volunteermatch.org or www.dosomething.org allow you to search charities by topic.

* Find out how the charity uses its money. Does most of it go to the people who need it? There are websites listed on page 47 that can help you find out.

* Once you have chosen a charity, find out what help it needs. Some are looking for volunteers, while others need donations of money or goods.

Talk with a trusted adult

Many of the young people featured in this book had help and support from their parents and other adults. No matter what you want to get involved with, you should discuss it with a parent, teacher, or club leader. Adults will help you stay safe. They can provide advice and check to see that any organization you want to help is worthy of your time and effort.

Stick together

We can all help each other with our own personal challenges—there is strength in numbers! Look out for people who are having a rough time. They may be able to return the favor one day. If you find a cause that you care about, see if your family, friends, or classmates will lend a hand.

Glossary

abolish make something illegal or stop it completely

birth certificate official document that shows a person's name and date of birth

cancer life-threatening illness caused by a tumor growing inside a person's body

civil war war between different groups of people within a country

Commonwealth Games sports competition between countries that are part of a group called the Commonwealth, which includes the United Kingdom, Australia, and India

conference large meeting held to discuss and present news on a particular issue

destiny something that is "meant to happen" in a person's life

determination commitment to work hard at something and not give up

disability physical or mental problem or difficulty

donate give as a gift, to help a person or project

extract part of a passage of writing

forced marriage marriage in which a couple's families make them take part

fund-raise collect money for a specific project

gang organized group of criminals with membership rules and codes of behavior

HIV/AIDS HIV is a virus that can cause a life-threatening illness, called AIDS

hospice type of hospital that cares for people who are dying or extremely sick

mainstream open to most people to attend

motivational speaker person who gives talks aimed to encourage and inspire others

petition protest that collects as many people's signatures as possible in support of a cause

poverty state of being extremely poor

private school school that people pay to go to

rappel method of lowering oneself on a rope from a height to the ground, such as from a cliff or tall building

refugee person who has had to flee his or her home because of war or a natural disaster

register enter in an official list

ritual practice that a person does over and over again

slavery situation in which people are kept as slaves and forced to work without pay or rights

social activist person who fights for and involves many others in a cause he or she believes in

sponsor give money to someone to take part in a event, which the person then gives to a good cause

tumor tissue in the body that keeps growing when it shouldn't

visually impaired have problems seeing

Find Out More

Books

Asgedom, Mawi. *The Code: The Five Secrets of Teen Success.* Boston: Little, Brown, 2003.

Asgedom, Mawi. *Of Beetles and Angels: A Boy's Remarkable Journey from a Refugee Camp to Harvard.* Boston: Little, Brown, 2002.

Hamilton, Bethany. *Soul Surfer: A True Story of Faith, Family, and Fighting to Get Back on the Board.* New York: Pocket, 2004.

Hudak, Heather C. *Oprah Winfrey* (Remarkable People). New York: Weigl, 2010.

Lynch, Emma. *Helen Keller* (Lives and Times). Chicago: Heinemann Library, 2005.

Websites

bethanyhamilton.com
This is the website of Bethany Hamilton, who lost her arm in a rare shark attack, but has gone on to become a champion surfer.

www.mawispeaks.com
Visit the website of Mawi Asgedom, who left his life in a refugee camp to become a Harvard graduate and best-selling author.

www.dosomething.org
www.idealist.org
www.volunteermatch.org
These three websites all help to match people with volunteer activities in their area or elsewhere.

www.charitynavigator.org
www.givewell.org
www2.guidestar.org
These three websites are useful places to go if you want to find out more about a particular charity or organization.

Index